A Message to Parents!
PRIVATE ZONE
should be read by
YOU FIRST

- so that you understand beforehand the development of the message and how to use it.
- so that the names you use to identify the parts of the PRIVATE ZONE are words both you and your child are comfortable with. Use of the proper anatomical terms is recommended.
- so that the book, which is suitable for ages three to nine, can be interpreted by you with regard for your child's emotional level as well as chronological age.

Arrange a quiet, unhurried time when you and your child READ TOGETHER

- so that you can be there to prevent your child from making incorrect assumptions from the pictures or text.
- so that you can answer questions fully when they arise.
- so that you can "play roles" without embarrassment.
- so that you are prepared to cope if you discover through discussion that your child has already been assaulted.

Intended as a general guide, PRIVATE ZONE does not give specific advice. It does not tell you, for example, how to deal with a friend or relative who has molested your child. It does, however, provide a hotline phone number to call to get the number of the counseling center in your area.

CONSULTANTS

Our sincere appreciation to the following for their suggestions and support in this project.

Kay Christy
Educational Consultant
Pierce County Rape Relief
Washington State Coalition of
  Sexual Assault Programs
Washington State

JoAnn Dunn, MSW, ACSW
Coordinator
Rape/Spouse Abuse Crisis
  Center
Family Service Assoc.
Lincoln, Nebraska

Gary Best, Ph.D.
Professor of Education
Dept. of Special Education
Calif. State University
Los Angeles, California

Marita D. Bausman, MA, CCMHC
Woonsocket Family and Child
  Services
Woonsocket, Rhode Island

Wayne Holder, ACSW
Director
American Humane Assoc.
Child Protection Division
Denver, Colorado

Donald L. Olauson and Staff
Office of Children, Youth and
  Family Services
Brookings, South Dakota

Laura Park
Elementary School Principal
Edmonds, Washington

Laurie Kaslow, MSW
Lois Glass, MSW
Boston Area Rape Crisis Center
Cambridge, Massachusetts

Gail Olson and Staff
Billings Rape Task Force
Billings, Montana

Kurt Weiss, MA
Information Specialist
Regional Institute of
  Social Welfare Research
Athens, Georgia

Marsha Silverman
Women's Committee on Sex Offenses
South Bend, Indiana

PRIVATE ZONE

A BOOK TEACHING CHILDREN
SEXUAL ASSAULT PREVENTION TOOLS

Frances S. Dayee

Foreword by Gary A. Best, Ph.D.,
Professor of Education, Certified Sex
Educator, AASECT, California State
University, Los Angeles

Illustrated by Marina Megale
Edited by Linda D. Meyer

WARNER BOOKS

A Warner Communications Company

To my loving family, especially Troy.

Text Copyright © 1982 by Frances S. Dayee
Illustrations Copyright © 1982 by Marina Megale

This Warner Books edition is published by arrangement with the author.

Warner Books, Inc., 666 Fifth Avenue, New York, NY 10103
A Warner Communications Company
Printed in the United States of America
First Warner printing: October 1984
10 9 8 7 6 5 4 3 2

Library of Congress Cataloging in Publication Data

Dayee, Frances S.
    Private zone.

    Reprint. Originally published: Edmonds, WA :
C. Franklin Press, 1982.
    Bibliography: p.
    Summary: A manual on understanding and prevention of
sexual abuse to be read by parents and children together.
    1. Child molesting—Prevention—Juvenile literature.
[1. Child molesting—Prevention.   2. Sex crimes—Pre-
vention.   3. Sex instruction for children.   4. Safety]
I. Meyer, Linda D. II. Marina Megale, ill.
III. Title.
HQ71.D25   1984   362.7'044   84-5144

ISBN 0-446-38053-9 (pbk.) (U.S.A.)
       0-446-38054-7 (pbk.) (Canada)

Foreword

Read PRIVATE ZONE. Use PRIVATE ZONE. If there
was ever a request that could be made of a reader that
somehow could be made a friendly command, it would
be found in the first two sentences above. We will probably
never know the impact this book will have on protecting
children from sexual assault. However, if only one child
is safer because he or she "yells and tells", then the efforts
taken in writing this book and the readers' efforts in using
it will be worthwhile.

Sexual abuse is somewhat analogous to the prospects
of a home fire or other catastrophe -- "It won't happen to
me!" While fires, floods, and accidents are not selective in
their victims, neither is there a selectivity in who may or
may not be sexually abused. The very young child, the
older adult, and even the person with a disability may
become victims.

The best protection against this personal violation is
education. PRIVATE ZONE is written in such a way that
it may become one of the most valuable teaching tools
available in the home, school, church or service agency.

The message of this book will be made stronger if the
adult and child together become familiar with and use the
correct language for sex education and protection.

Learning is less of a mystery for children when they are told correct names of body parts and the facts of functioning rather than being beseiged with incorrect names which will eventually need to be unlearned with the appropriate language introduced at a later time. The goal of this book is protection. Infantile language hardly seems appropriate for a topic that is far from cute.

There are no guarantees to be made from the use of PRIVATE ZONE. But responsible adults who use it will have the satisfaction of knowing that they have contributed to the safety, protection, and education of our most valuable asset: our children.

Gary A. Best, Ph.D
Professor of Education
Certified Sex Educator, AASECT
California State University
Los Angeles, California

Adult's Page

Sexual assault of children is a vitally important and frightening subject. It is not rare. Chances are every person will feel the impact of this experience either personally or through friends or family.

Statistics indicate one out of every four girls and one out of ten boys is sexually assaulted before age eighteen.* This does not begin to tell the whole story, as this study did not include an assault case unless the offender was at least five years older than the victim.

Even more distressing is the fact that in 85% of reported assaults, children are not victimized by a stranger but by someone they know.

Sexual assault of children ranges from an adult showing a child his or her genitals, to oral sex or penetration.

The earlier children learn the facts about this subject, the better their chances of being protected from the experience. **Informed children are safer children.**

The purpose of this "read aloud" book is: 1) to create an atmosphere of open discussion about a delicate subject in a non-frightening way, 2) to give children tools to use as preventive measures against sexual assault, 3) to give

* The Kinsey Report - Alfred C. Kinsey -
  Vol. I: Sexual Behavior in the Human Female
  Vol. II: Sexual Behavior in the Human Male

children an aid in recognizing trouble signs, 4) to guard against repeated assaults, and 5) to teach children recognition and reporting skills if sexual assault situations occur.

The decision to be more specific about correct names for genitals, anus, chest and breasts is left to adult discretion because of the age group for whom this book is intended and the variety of situations in which it may be used.

However, the use of proper anatomical terms is encouraged. The more specific an adult is, the better equipped children are to handle, recognize and/or explain sexual assault.

Although the language is simple enough for children to understand, adults are encouraged to impress upon children: 1) the different parts of the private zone, 2) who can touch the private zones, 3) the difference between 'good touching' and 'bad touching', and 4) the importance of children's telling responsible adults if they are threatened by or experience sexual assault.

Also, please consider, if the children are told to tell, they will tell, since what this book teaches is assertiveness. It is not meant to usurp parental authority but to protect the child. Positive reinforcement of telling is important as a negative reaction may embarrass or frighten and cause children to reject this tool. Therefore, a discussion on telling may be useful. This might be accomplished by play-acting situations to test and increase children's understanding.

Unfortunately, the sexual assault of children is a reality that won't automatically go away if we just refuse to face it or talk about it. Purposeful education about the topic is the chance to provide children with the information they need to recognize the dangers and characteristics of assault. Although there are no guarantees, INFORMED CHILDREN ARE SAFER CHILDREN.

PRIVATE ZONE

The Read-Together Picture Story

This is Tommy!
This is Susie!
They are going to the beach. They are wearing bathing suits to the beach.

Do you know what bathing suits cover? Bathing suits cover special parts of the body called the PRIVATE ZONE. The parts of your body your bathing suit covers is your PRIVATE ZONE.

You have a PRIVATE ZONE. Big people like Mommies and Daddies have PRIVATE ZONES. Big kids and small kids that go to school have PRIVATE ZONES. Tommy and Susie have PRIVATE ZONES. Even babies have PRIVATE ZONES.

The only thing in the whole wide world
that everybody has is a body with a
PRIVATE ZONE.

Everybody doesn't have a big beach
ball. Everybody doesn't have a bike.
Everybody doesn't have a dog. But,
everybody's body has a PRIVATE ZONE.

Where is your PRIVATE ZONE? Did you notice it's not just one big spot? A PRIVATE ZONE has many different parts.

Do you know what private means?

Private means it's all yours. No one may touch it unless you say they may.

Some people have a whole bedroom that is all theirs and no one may come in unless they say it's okay. Tommy has a shelf that is all his. He puts special things like his blanket on it. Susie has a drawer that is all hers. She keeps her special school papers in it. Big people usually have letters they say are private. Most people have toothbrushes that belong only to them.

Can you think of something of yours that is private?

When something is private and your brother, sister or friend touches it, you may say, "Don't touch. That's mine." If they touch it anyway, you may tell your Mommy or Daddy. Since parents usually know when something is private, they will understand and can talk to your brother, sister, or friend.

Even Mommies and Daddies know they aren't supposed to touch your private belongings because they are private and belong to you.

Do you know what zone means?

A zone is a place set aside for a special reason. A bus zone is a place for people to wait for the bus. A school zone is the part around the school where people in cars are supposed to drive slowly. Can you think of some other zones?

Now I bet you figured out what
PRIVATE ZONE means.

Do you know <u>who</u> can touch your
PRIVATE ZONE?

<u>You</u> can touch your PRIVATE ZONE.

If you hurt a part of your PRIVATE
ZONE, Mommy or Daddy may put medicine
on it to make it feel better. Mommy or
Daddy might touch your PRIVATE ZONE

if they are helping you take a bath, or helping you get cleaned up. If you don't need help, you have the right to say, "Thank you. I can do it myself."

Have you ever seen a baby make a big mess and need his or her diaper changed? Messy babies sure need help. A big person who is changing a diaper can touch the baby's PRIVATE ZONE to clean him up.

But big people, even Mommies and Daddies, need a good reason for touching a PRIVATE ZONE because it is private.

When you go to see the doctor with your Mommy and Daddy, a doctor might need to touch your PRIVATE ZONE. Some children need to have their temperatures taken in a part of their PRIVATE ZONE. Sometimes you get a shot in your PRIVATE ZONE. Ouch! Perhaps you need to go to the doctor because some part of your PRIVATE ZONE hurts.

But even a doctor or nurse needs a good reason to touch your PRIVATE ZONE because it's private and it belongs to you.

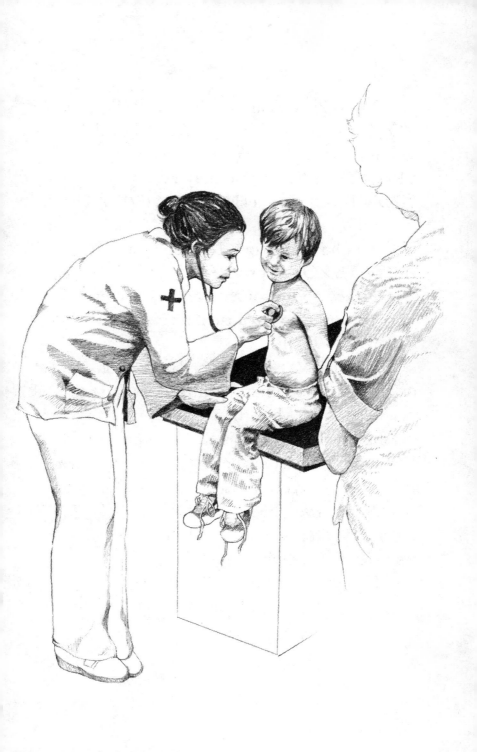

Nobody else can touch your PRIVATE ZONE. Not even your friends. If they do, you may say, "Don't touch. That's my PRIVATE ZONE." You may even yell, "DON'T TOUCH! THAT'S MY PRIVATE ZONE!"

You have the right to keep your PRIVATE ZONE, <u>private</u>.

If they try to touch it anyway, you may tell on them because it's <u>your</u> PRIVATE ZONE.

Your PRIVATE ZONE belongs to you—and only to you. More than Tommy's private shelf belongs to him. More than Susie's private drawer belongs to her. Even more than Mommy's and Daddy's private letters belong to them. It's more private than anything else of yours—even your toothbrush. Everybody has a PRIVATE ZONE, but yours is especially important to you because it's part of your own body.

I bet you knew that!

But, did you know that your PRIVATE ZONE is even more important than candy? Or that it's even more important than secrets?

Did you know that if someone touches your PRIVATE ZONE and they say, "You will get into trouble if you tell," you haven't done anything wrong? You may tell a policeman or doctor or best friend, and you won't get into trouble.

If someone asks you to touch his or her PRIVATE ZONE and then says, "You're bad," it's not true. It's not your fault. You aren't bad, and you may still tell. Mommies, Daddies and grandparents would want you to tell.

If a person just asks you to show them your PRIVATE ZONE, you may yell and tell. You may yell and tell if they show you their PRIVATE ZONE. Even if they say, "It's our secret," you may yell and tell. That kind of secret should never be a secret. For sure you have the right to yell and tell.

You can tell a teacher or babysitter or anybody in the whole wide world until someone listens and helps you. Did you know that? You sure can.

A PRIVATE ZONE is the only thing in the whole wide world everybody has. Everybody in the whole wide world has the right to keep his or her PRIVATE ZONE, private.

Especially you!

SEXUAL ASSAULT INDICATORS

Children go through stages normally, but if two or
more of these symptoms appear simultaneously, investigate.

Personality change

Outgoing child becomes clingy

Changes in toilet training habits

Signs of being uncomfortable with someone
    formerly trusted

Child withdraws into self

Child talks about sex acts without having had prior
knowledge (movies, TV, instruction)

Moody, cries excessively

Changes in eating, sleeping habits

Increased activity

Behavior problems

Unusual shyness

Sudden unfounded fears

Child has unusual need for "you're O.K."
    reassurance

Child shows unnatural interest in own
    or other's genitals

Social skills change

IF A CHILD IS SEXUALLY ASSAULTED

1. **BELIEVE THE CHILD**
   Specialists who work with sexually abused children report children do not lie about sexual assault.

2. **STAY CALM**
   Shock, anger, fear, guilt, shame and disbelief are normal reactions, especially when the offender is someone you and/or the child trusted. This emotional turmoil adversely affects the child. You shouldn't bottle up emotions, however; allow yourself to cry, stomp or throw things in private.

3. **REASSURE THE CHILD**
   Maybe something like this: "Thank you for sharing this experience with me. You are such a good girl/boy. I'm proud of you for telling me! I'm sorry you had a bad experience with an adult. Sometimes even adults do bad things, but you didn't do anything bad. You did just the right thing when you told me. It wasn't your fault. I'll protect you. Thank you for coming to me. I love you."

4. **SEEK HELP**
   Child protective services, child abuse agencies, rape relief centers and sexual assault centers around the United States and Canada usually have specialists for child victims of assault. If a center is not available in your community, talk to your family physician. A doctor may be in a good position to locate help for you and your child.

NATIONAL CHILD ABUSE HOTLINE - REFERRAL
SERVICE 1-800-4AC-HILD
1-800-422-4453

5. **IF THE CHILD BRINGS IT UP, TALK ABOUT THE ASSAULT.**

   Let the child talk about what happened and continue to reassure him/her. If the child is not allowed to talk about it, she/he has a tendency to blame him/herself. Don't underestimate the importance of reassuring the child. Even after repeated assurances, when a four-year-old was asked if he would talk to the police, he asked, "Will they put me in jail too?"

6. **TAKE ACTION**

   In 99 out of 100 cases the offender is a repeater. In the past legal action was nearly impossible, especially when the victims were six and under. Now, in some areas, an advocate can testify on behalf of the child.

7. **IF THE OFFENDER IS A FRIEND OR LOVED ONE:**

   A child doesn't want to get a friend or loved one into trouble. Let the child know your intention is not to put the offender into jail, but to get him/her help. Consult a specialist at a sexual assault center, a psychologist or a psychiatrist to help you to confront the offender and handle the problems that can arise from the confrontation.

ADDITIONAL READING

CHILD SEXUAL ASSAULT PREVENTION PROJECT: An Educational Program for Children by Cordelia Kent, 1979.

Curriculum for elementary and secondary teachers. The Touch Continuum which is introduced is used as a basis for much of the recent prevention work. Discusses different kinds of touch, ranging from nurturing/caring to hurtful/exploitive touch.

120pp
Hennepin County Sexual Assault Services
2000-C Government Center
Minneapolis, MN 55487

HE TOLD ME NOT TO TELL by King County Rape Relief, 1979.

A collection of suggestions to be used by parents or teachers when talking about child sexual assault. Preventive ideas and examples of how children can report assault are included.

28pp
King County Rape Relief
305 S. 43rd
Renton, WA 98055

MY VERY OWN BOOK ABOUT ME by Jo Stowell and Mary Dietzel, 1980.

A color book/workbook for children, it uses the concepts of the body's private parts and "ok/not ok touch". Written text provides a wealth of information for children and establishes a child's abilities and personal rights.

39pp
Spokane Rape Crisis Center
Lutheran Social Services
North 1226 Howard
Spokane, WA 99201

NO MORE SECRETS: Protecting Your Child From Sexual Assault by Caren Adams and Jennifer Fay, 1981.

Excellent book for parents on how to talk with children about sexual assault. Examples of actual words or phrases are used to ease discomfort in discussing the topic. Emphasis is placed on a child's right to control who touches them and telling about inappropriate touching. Included are: prevention games to play with children, indicators of potentially dangerous situations, and supportive information to parents who have been victimized.

90pp
Impact Publishers
P.O. Box 1094
San Luis Obispo, CA 93406

PUBLIC EDUCATION MANUAL, Project Coordinator: Kay Christy, Technical Writer: Carolyn March, 1982.

Designed for sexual assault prevention educators, it includes the organization and management of a speaking component, training speakers, developing a presentation, and state and national resources.

Washington Coalition of Sexual Assault Programs
1063 Capital Way S. #217
Olympia, WA 98501

RED FLAG, GREEN FLAG PEOPLE by Joy Williams, 1980.

A coloring book for children ages 3-10 years, this book focuses on the dangerous stranger and is not clear about what may happen to children. One situation does involve a relative.

22pp
Rape and Abuse Crisis Center
P.O. Box 1655
Fargo, N.D. 58107

SEXUAL ABUSE OF CHILDREN: Selected Readings by the National Center on Child Abuse and Neglect, 1980.

A compilation of 19 articles by various people in the field of child sexual abuse, it covers topics such as short term management of sexual abuse and incest treatment, interviewing techniques, medical protocol, sexual exploitation and etiology.

193 pp
Region X Child Abuse/Neglect Resource Center
157 Yesler Way, #208
Seattle, WA 98104

SEXUAL MISUSE OF CHILDREN: Tools for Understanding by Kay Christy, 1978.

This manual which focuses toward educators and parents, includes several exercises to be used with children. A clear discussion of the definitions and misconceptions surrounding sexual misuse and incest is emphasized.

51pp
Pierce County Rape Relief
Allenmore Medical Center #B-2002
19th and Union
Tacoma, WA 98405

THE SILENT CHILDREN: A Book For Parents About Prevention of Child Abuse by Linda Sanford, McGraw-Hill

Provides clear background on the sexual abuse of children. Recommended for the parent without much information about the issues. Focuses on prevention techniques as well as exercises. Developing self-awareness, esteem, and confidence are emphasized.

367pp, paperback

SOMETIMES I NEED TO SAY NO! by Lisa W. Strick.

A series of short skits designed for children to observe using songs and humor. The concept is based on a privacy continuum and moves from the general to specific issues of sexual assault. Included are supplemental activities for teachers, parents, and kids.

Rape Crisis Center of Syracuse
423 W. Onandaga St.
Syracuse, NY 13203

STUDY CARDS - TOUCH CONTINUUM

Thirteen cards measuring 14" x 22" with examples of different kinds of touch on one side and discussion suggestions on the other side. Intended for grades K-8 as a classroom tool and visual aid. Would complement other sexual abuse prevention education.

13 cards
Illusion Theatre
528 Hennipin Ave. #309
Minneapolis, MN 55403

COME TELL ME RIGHT AWAY: A Positive Approach to Warning Children About Sexual Abuse by Linda Sanford

A comforting approach to helping parents talk to children about sexual assault. A confidence builder. Example conversations are warm and friendly and follow through.

24pp
Linda Sanford
123 Sutherland Road
Brookline, MA 02146

SEX EDUCATION

YOUR CHILD SHOULD KNOW by Flora Colao and Tamar Hosansky

A book by the founders of the Safety and Fitness Exchange (SAFE) in New York City, which offers personal safety programs for schools, agencies and such groups as the Girl Scouts and the Crisis Club. A distillation of the advice on prevention and treatment after sexual assault they have offered to parents and children in their workshops and seminars.

160 pp
The Bobbs-Merrill Company, Inc.
P.O. Box 7083
Indianapolis, IN 46206

Author's Biography

Frances S. Dayee is a native of Washington State and resides in Seattle with her husband and thirteen children.

When one of her children was sexually assaulted, she realized how ignorant she was about the subject. It shocked her that her four-year-old boy was the victim, he was playing in his own backyard, he was alone only five minutes before his disappearance was discovered, and, worst of all, he was assaulted by a close family friend.

"I felt like I'd been deceiving my children. I had warned them about strangers, not friends. But how do you tell children that without frightening them?"

That's how "PRIVATE ZONE", a book for young children, was born. "The earlier children learn the facts about sexual assault, the better their defenses. Informed children are safer children."